AF504038

1.

David Downe

'We call Learners Novices Officer.'

Nimmo's Choice

A COLLECTION OF CARTOONS

Compiled and Introduced by
DEREK NIMMO

MOWBRAYS LONDON & OXFORD

FOREWORD

I was most intrigued when I was invited to select the cartoons
contained within this little book. It was only when they arrived and I
began to rummage through them that it occurred to me that over
the last few years I have practically become an ecclesiastical
caricature myself. Since 1965 I have appeared on television and
radio in assorted ecclesiastical comedy series. In one year in fact I
played an Anglican vicar fourteen times and a Catholic monk seven.
Once, memorably, on Christmas Day, I played a nun as well—a
sight it was said that was nearly enough to make Danny La Rue
reach for his trousers.

In my experience however the hazards of appearing both in
Protestant and Catholic series are, one can only say, manifold.
During the last series of 'Oh Brother' for instance I happened to be
filming in St Peter's Square in Rome. Whilst the cameras were
being set up I wandered away in my monastic robes to inspect the
great Basilica. En route I met a very charming Englishman who
stopped me and asked whether I would mind having my
photograph taken with his equally charming daughter. There
seemed to be no particular hazard involved so I put one arm . . . or
perhaps two . . . around her and he happily snapped away. As I
started to return to my film unit, I felt a very unfriendly hand on my
shoulder. When I turned round I discovered that it belonged to the
equally unfriendly arm of a Vatican policeman. He indicated that I
was to accompany him and, as his companion was one of those
Swiss Guard chaps carrying a very long spike, I decided I had little
choice. I was taken across the square and put into a singularly
dreary cell, somewhere beneath the Curia. It was there that I
discovered that I had been 'shopped', I believe the word is, by a nun.
Apparently she had decided that by wrapping my arms around a
young lady I was not only behaving in a thoroughly unmonkly way
but was also most decidedly carrying Christian love far too far. The
police demanded to know my identity. I told them I was an actor
which didn't impress them terribly and then that I was working with
the BBC, which seemed to impress them still less. They then went

to look for my film crew but my gallant producer, seeing my arrest, had fled back to the hotel, taking the unit with him. Unfortunately the Chief of Police turned out to be an Anglophobe of the first order. Whilst serving in the Italian Army he had been captured by the British in the Western Desert and had then spent the rest of the war working on a potato farm near Wigan. This experience seemed to have soured him. My trouble was that I had absolutely no way of proving my identity. I had to wear this rather grotty robe (the real monks these days wear lovely silk and mohair outfits) a thick crucifix and some rather ill-chosen rosary beads, whilst on my head rested the BBC issue pink plastic tonsure, held on by ladies' hair grips. This last mentioned object seemed to offend them most and it was removed from my head and placed on the Police Station table—to act as Exhibit A.

I then became even more pompous than usual and demanded to see my Consul and/or Ambassador—all to no avail. My producer refused to answer the telephone and as they seemed to be getting rather bored with me, they popped me back into my cell. Some eight hours later a rather timely miracle happened in the shape of an Irish Dominican monk. He had just returned from leave to Co. Cork and presumably had spent the time locked to his sister's television, for he was able to account for me. The Chief of Police then turned decidedly more cheery, my release was arranged, they took away my robes, handed me a blanket and told me not to make a habit of it.

Having made good my get away from the Eternal City, I came back to continue filming in England. Within moments of the cameras beginning to turn, I was hit in the face with an ecclesiastical plank. This whacked me hard round the face, removed a couple of teeth and blacked one eye. I was taken to the nearest hostpital where the Indian doctor who examined me had only recently arrived from Delhi. He asked me to tell him exactly what had happened. I had a go.

'Well doctor,' I said as he wrote it all down, 'I was in this church do you see, standing on a plank balanced on a log in front of the altar.' For some reason he asked me to repeat this. I did. 'And then doctor, there were these two fat monks standing on top of the altar.' 'Did you say MONKS?' he asked. 'Well actually I did, and these two monks jumped off the top of the altar on to the end of the plank in the hope of sending me up . . .' 'Sending you up?' 'Yes, that is exactly right, sending me up into the air so that I could grab hold of the chandelier.' 'What chandelier was that?' 'The one in the church that I intended swinging on but it didn't work out that way. When the monks jumped, the plank slew round and bashed me, as you can see.' At this point, curiously enough, the doctor decided to stop writing.

One thing however that has always delighted me about the series is the small amount of offence that they seem to have occasioned, and never ever to the clergy themselves. I suppose that the reason for this is that, like the cartoons that are within this book, we have always laughed with the Church rather than laughing at it. Again like this book, it is never suggested that the characters within the plays are in any way unchristian, only fallible. In fact in all these years I have only ever received two mildly grumbling letters from the professional religious. The first was from a Baptist minister who wrote saying that there had been a Catholic comedy series, 'Oh Father', and an Anglican one, 'All Gas and Gaiters', but he could not see why the non-conformist church had been completely neglected —which on the face of it seems to be masochism run wild. The other letter which was in a similar vein came from a Salvation Army Captain, who wrote actually enclosing some scripts and saying what an excellent subject the Salvation Army would be for a comedy programme. He might be right too—I rather fancy myself with a tambourine.

Much more typical was the reaction of the Prior of the Carmelite Priory Gort Muire, Dublin, which I recently revisited, whose only comment was that whilst he liked 'All Gas and Gaiters' he much preferred my monastic series 'Oh Brother' because he said 'That's how it really goes on here'. The good Prior incidentally is I suppose the Jimmy Tarbuck of the monastic world, which can best be illustrated by his opening greeting to me when I returned to Ireland. His very first line was, 'It is nice to see you again my son, nice to see you. Have you heard this one? Do you know the definition of homogeneous?' 'No Father,' said I, 'I'm afraid I don't.' 'Well Derek it is a poof with a degree.'

I am sure he will laugh at the cartoons, I hope you will too.

INDEX to ARTISTS

Photoset, printed and bound
in Great Britain by
REDWOOD BURN LIMITED
Trowbridge & Esher

ISBN 0 264 66083 8

First published 1974

A. R. Mowbray & Co Ltd, The Alden Press, Osney Mead, Oxford, OX2 OEG

2.   *James D. Crocker*

'I've doubled my flock since I became a United supporter!'

3.   *R. Vinson*

4.   *R. Vinson*

'And remember to buy a new tea cosy tomorrow dear.'

5.   *James D. Crocker*

'Father – not Daddy – you fool!'

6.   *A. F. Ralley*

7.   *G. G. Walker*

8. *James D. Crocker*

'Sunday morning – back to the grind-stone!'

9. *K. Bartlam*

'Hello operator – I want a long distance parson to parson call!'

10.

J. Field

11.   *T. Bayley-Hughes*

'You've got to admit that his sermons are
always topical!'

12.   *T. Bayley-Hughes*

'Brother Nathaniel worked on the farm
before coming to us!'

13.   *Colin Earl*

'. . . I do!'

14.   *K. Bartlam*

'I'm her first husband — here's a list of don'ts!'

15.   A. F. Ralley

'It's little Bo Peep to see you dad.'

16.   A. F. Ralley

17.

Allan Gardham

18.   *James D. Crocker*

'He's an Auzzie!'

19.   'They say he was an Olympic gold medallist.'

'Blackleg.'

'Fifty per cent of our members are still above the poverty line.'

s protesting against vows of silence.'

'Demarcation — I do Gothic Capitals.'

David Downe

'The Management will see you now.'

21.   *T. Bayley-Hughes*

22.   *Bill Bowden*

  – Oh, it's not such a bad place – once you get into the
habit!'

23.   K. Bartlam

'Here's a good one to send to the Bishop!'

24.   D. Baker

'Isn't this the man who falls asleep during your sermons, dear?'

25.   J. B. Lawry

26.   T. Bayley-Hughes
'Have you read the book, Vicar?'

27.   A. F. Ralley
'A half of shandy, and a B . . . L . . . O . . . O
. . . D . . . Y mary please.'

28.   D. Baker

'Come in and take a pew.'

29. *G. G. Walker*

'What on earth gave you the idea that an archdeacon automatically becomes an archangel!'

30. *Bill Bowden*

'Dad, is that what they mean by "Taking Holy Orders"?'

31.   Colin Earl

32.   D. Baker

'See you later, dear, I'm just popping down to the pub.'

.33.

James D. Crocker

'Let us prey. . . .'

34.

Brian Platt

'I believe he's going electric, next week . . . !'

35.   A. F. Ralley

'I hate these amateurs.'

36.   J. B. Lawry

'We're filming a cookery programme.'

37.   R. Vinson

38.

D. Baker

39. *T. Bayley-Hughes*

'I enjoy your sermons very much, Vicar
— we didn't know what sin was until you
came here.'

40. *Bill Bowden*

— closed orders? I'll say it's a closed order — I've been here
since nineteen twenty-eight, and I only came to clear the
drains!'

41. *K. Bartlam*

'How many times must I tell you not to phone me at work, Mabel!'

42. *Dicky Howett*

'You're getting into some strange habits, Brother Boris!'

43.   *James D. Crocker*

'G'night, Charlie!'

44.   *G. G. Walker*

'Women!'

45.   *David Downe*

'Milk and honey, honey and milk ever since we got to the
promised land!'

46.   *Terry Reid*

'For heaven's sake, Torquil, cheer up!'

47.   Colin Earl

48.   J. B. Lawry
'I hate winter christenings!'

49.   *Allan Gardham*

'We believe in being prepared for all contingencies!

50.   *Francis R. Finch*

'With all your heart, with all your mind, with all your soul and with all your strength — without, of course, going to extremes.'

51.   *Francis R. Finch*

'If that one's too obviously Tillichian and the other is excessively dispensational, why not settle for straight exegesis?'

52.   *David Parry* .

'Dis train is bound for glory, dis train . . . !'

53.   *V. E. Cox / R. Poulter*

'Sorry son – you'll have to ask your mother.'

54.   D. Baker

'Are you quite sure your name is Smith?'

55.   K. Bartlam

'Who has been sending in anonymous requests for a double
cell!'

56.   *Colin Earl*

57.   *Brian Platt*

'. . . how did you know I was Un-orthodox . . .?'

58.   K. Bartlam

'This is a day I will never forget, Darling!'

59.   K. Bartlam

'Mother said this would be the most beautiful night of my life
and I don't want to miss a moment of it!'

60.

Colin Earl

61.   *J. B. Lawry*

'It's the wife's idea.'

62.   *R. W. Genney*

63.

Colin Earl

64.

James D. Crocker

'I got it at the Army Surplice Stores.'

65.   D. Baker

66.   Miss J. Capon

67.   *Francis R. Finch*

'Yes – I can share an insight with you, Guv, – Arkle for the three-thirty.'

68.   *D. Baker*

'Yes, I think women ought to be ordained – provided sermons are abolished.'

69.   T. Bayley-Hughes

'His appeal paid off better than I thought!'

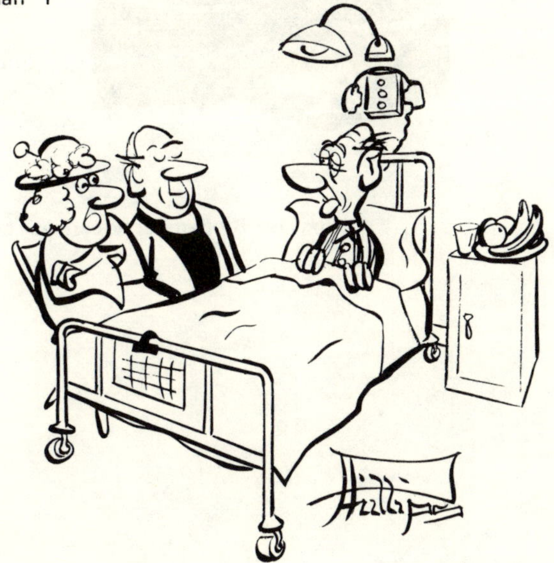

70.   A. C. Phillips

'I was only saying to Henry today, it's weeks since he did a funeral!'

71.   *Allan Gardham*

'If nothing else, Brother Cedric certainly believes in life before death.'

72.   *Francis R. Finch*

'Go on, be a trend setter.'

73.   *T. Bayley-Hughes*

'I had a feeling that that would pack them in !'

74.   *T. Bayley-Hughes*

'Tell you what, Sir — how about one pair for work and one for
the rest of the week!'

75.   *Bill Bowden*

'— grant you it's fast, but it'll never replace the quill!'

76.   *James D. Crocker*

'When is it my turn to get lost?'

77.   *A. C. Phillips*

'Sorry Sir – you can't come in without a tie!'

78.

'Complimentary!'

J. Field

79.   *Dicky Howett*

'Read me one of your sermons dear. I
can't get to sleep.'

80.   *Colin Earl*

81.   James D. Crocker